First Steps in Rational Emotive Behaviour Therapy for Clients

First Steps in Rational Emotive Behaviour Therapy for Clients

Second Edition

Windy Dryden

Rationality Publications

Rationality Publications
136 Montagu Mansions, London W1U 6LQ

www.rationalitypublications.com
info@rationalitypublications.com

Second edition published by Rationality Publications
Copyright (c) 2025 Windy Dryden

First edition published by the Albert Ellis Institute in 2006

ISBN: 978-1-914938-43-6

Contents

Introduction

I have written this small guide for clients who have started working with an REBT therapist. It is designed to help you use several important steps as you identify, assess and address specific emotional/behavioural problems. Throughout this guide, if you have questions or doubts about any of the material, discuss them with your REBT therapist.

Before you go through these steps, I need to explain REBT's *Situational ABCDE* framework. This framework will help you to understand what you need to focus on and change as you go about the business of helping yourself with REBT.

The *Situational ABCDE* Model of REBT

The *Situational ABCDE* model has six components: (1) *Situation*; (2) *A*; (3) *B;* (4) *C*; (5) *D* and (6) *E*. I will discuss these one at a time.

Situation

You do not experience an emotional problem in a vacuum. Rather there is almost always a *Situation* in which you experience this problem. In considering this *Situation*, remember that it should reflect as accurately as possible the context in which you experienced your emotional problem.

A

When you experience an emotional problem in the *Situation* that you are in, you usually disturb yourself about a particular aspect of this *Situation*. In REBT, we call this the *A* or adversity.

A is often an inference

It is important to appreciate that your *A* (or adversity) is usually an inference that you have made about the *Situation* or some aspect of the *Situation*. An inference goes beyond the data at hand and can be accurate or inaccurate. Thus, if you receive a note from your boss that they want to see you after lunch and you think: *My boss is going to criticise my work*, then this thought is an inference since it goes beyond the facts of the *Situation*. In this example, the facts are that your boss wants to see you after lunch. You do not know why. Your inference may be accurate or it may be inaccurate, but what makes it an inference is that it goes beyond the data at hand.

A relates to your personal domain

An adversity (real or inferred) is usually related to some aspect of your *personal domain*. The term *personal domain* was first introduced by Aaron Temkin Beck, the founder of cognitive therapy (an approach to cognitive-behaviour therapy which shares certain ideas with REBT). Your personal domain comprises people, objects, concepts and ideas that are important to you. It also contains what is important to you about yourself. When you experience different unhealthy negative emotions, you disturb yourself about different adversities within your personal domain. I discuss this further in point 2.4.

B

B stands for basic attitudes.[1] In REBT, these basic attitudes can be rigid and extreme or flexible and non-extreme.

Rigid/extreme attitudes and emotional disturbance

As mentioned above, REBT's position on the major determinants of emotional problems can be summed up as follows: People are disturbed not by adversities, but by the rigid and extreme basic attitudes that they hold towards these adversities. In REBT, these rigid and extreme basic attitudes are placed under *B* in the *Situational ABCDE* model. For example, a threat to your personal domain at *A* does not make you anxious. Rather you make yourself anxious by holding a rigid/extreme attitude at *B* towards this threat.

Rigid and extreme attitudes have the following characteristics. They are inconsistent with reality, illogical or nonsensical, and largely unconstructive in their consequences.

Flexible/non-extreme attitudes and emotional health

REBT's position on emotional health can also be summed up thus: People can respond healthily to adversities by holding flexible and non-extreme basic attitudes towards these adversities. In REBT, these flexible and non-extreme attitudes are also placed under *B* in the *Situational ABCDE* model. Thus, you are concerned, but not anxious about a threat to your personal domain at *A* because you hold a flexible/non-extreme attitude at *B* towards this threat.

Flexible and non-extreme attitudes have the following characteristics. They are consistent with reality, logical or sensible, and largely constructive in their consequences.

---

[1] In this guide, I will most often refer to these basic attitudes as attitudes.

Four rigid/extreme and flexible/non-extreme attitudes

REBT theory posits four rigid/extreme attitudes and four alternative flexible/non-extreme attitudes. These are summarised in Table 1 (next page), but I will discuss them further later in this guide.

C

When you hold an attitude towards an adversity, REBT recognises that there are major consequences (at C) of holding this attitude.

Three major consequences of an attitude

When using REBT, particularly look for three major consequences of holding an attitude at B.

- Emotional
- Behavioural
- Thinking

CONSEQUENCES OF HOLDING A RIGID/EXTREME ATTITUDE. The influence of holding a rigid/extreme attitude on your emotions, behaviour and subsequent thinking can be summed up as follows:

> When you face an adversity, and you hold a rigid/extreme attitude towards this adversity, the consequences of doing so are likely to be as follows:
>
> - *C* (emotional) = Largely negative and unhealthy
> - *C* (behavioural) = Largely dysfunctional
> - *C* (thinking) = Highly distorted and skewed to the negative

Table 1 Four rigid/extreme attitudes and four flexible/non-extreme attitudes

Rigid/Extreme Attitudes	Flexible/Non-Extreme Attitudes
Rigid Attitude • I would like X to happen (or not happen and therefore, it must be the way I want it to be	**Flexible Attitude** • I would like X to happen (or not happen), but it does not have to be the way I want it to be
Awfulising Attitude • It would be bad if X happens (or does not happen), and therefore, it would be terrible	**Non-Awfulising Attitude** • It would be bad if X happens)or does not happen, but it would not be terrible.
Unbearability Attitude • I would struggle to bear it if X happens (or does not happen), and therefore I could not bear it	**Bearability Attitude** • I would struggle to bear it if X happens (or does not happen), but: - I could bear it - It would be worth it to me to bear it - I am worth bearing it for - I am willing to bear it - I am going to bear it - This is what I am going to do to bear it
Devaluation Attitude • If X happens (or does not happen), I would be no good; you would be no good; life would be no good	**Unconditional Acceptance Attitude** • If X happens (or does not happen), it would not prove that I am no good; you are no good; life is no good. It would prove that I am/you are a complex, fallible human being and that life is a complex mixture of good, bad and neutral features

As this is a beginner's guide to REBT, I will focus largely on your emotional *Cs*, although I will also discuss your behavioural *Cs*. I will not discuss thinking *Cs* here, but your REBT therapist will raise this issue with you as appropriate.

CONSEQUENCES OF HOLDING A FLEXIBLE/NON-EXTREME ATTITUDE. The influence of holding flexible/non-extreme attitudes on your emotions, behaviours and subsequent thinking can be summed up as follows:

When you face an adversity, and you hold a flexible/non-extreme attitude towards this adversity, the consequences of doing so are likely to be as follows:

- *C* (emotional) = Largely negative and healthy
- *C* (behavioural = Largely functional
- *C* (thinking)   = Largely realistic and balanced

D

In REBT theory, *D* stands for a dialectical examination of attitudes. This means that at the appropriate time, you will take your rigid/extreme attitude and alternative flexible/non-extreme attitudes, which demonstrate opposite views and examine them to arrive at the truth. As I will discuss the dialectical examination of attitudes[2] fully in Step 4 of this guide, I will not go into further detail here.

E

E stands for the effects of examining attitudes. When this process is successful, you will experience healthy (rather than unhealthy)

---

[2] Henceforth, I will use the term examination rather than 'dialectical examination'.

negative emotions about life's adversities. These healthy negative emotions will help you to change life's adversities if they can be changed or to adjust constructively to them if they cannot be changed.

Having introduced you to REBT's *Situational ABCDE* model, you are ready to deal with your emotional/behavioural problems. In REBT, we argue that this is best done by focusing on your problems one at a time. Therefore, this guide has been written to help you identify, assess and address one of your problems.

STEP 1

Define Your Nominated Problem and Be Goal-Oriented

1.1   Choose one problem to work on

You may have several problems, but as I have said, REBT works best when you focus on one problem at a time.

So ask yourself:

- ***What problem would I like to focus on?***[3]

When you have chosen a problem – which is known in REBT as your nominated problem – stick with it as you go through the steps outlined in this guide.

---

[3] All such questions in this guide are illustrative.

1.2   Describe your nominated problem

State your nominated problem as clearly as you can. A good description contains your disturbed feelings (at *C* in the *ABCDE* framework) and what adversity (at *A*) you feel disturbed about.

I feel ……. (C) whenever ……. (*A*)

For example:

- *I feel anxious (C) whenever I think I may be criticised (A)*
- *I feel guilty (C) whenever I think I have upset someone (A)*

1.3   Assess for the presence of a meta-emotional problem and decide if this is to become your nominated problem

Having disturbed yourself in the first place, being human, you may disturb yourself about your original disturbance. In REBT, this is known as a meta-emotional problem (literally an emotional problem about an emotional problem or a behavioural problem).

Ask yourself:

How do I feel about … (state your original emotional/behavioural problem)?

If you do have a meta-emotional problem, you need to decide which of your two problems – the original emotional/behavioural problem or the meta-emotional problem – will be your nominated problem, the one that will become the focus of your self-help. My advice is that you focus on your original emotional/behavioural problem unless:

• You want to work on your meta-emotional problem first.
• The existence of your meta-emotional problem will interfere with you focusing on your original emotional/behavioural problem in a therapy session.
• The existence of your meta-emotional problem will interfere with you working on your original emotional/behavioural problem in your life.

If you are unsure about this, discuss it with your REBT therapist.

1.4   Establish a goal-orientation

If you have described your nominated problem in general terms, you need to establish a goal-oriented orientation. In doing so, understand that you need to react healthily to the adversity at *A* before trying to change it directly. Setting a general goal direction is acceptable at this point. You will set specific goals later (see Appendix 1).

Ask yourself:

• *What would I like to achieve from focusing on this problem?*

If you want to change a *Situation* or another person, realise this is not an acceptable goal in REBT. This is because neither *Situations* nor other people are under your direct control. However, you can change your own behaviour which may have a positive impact on the *Situation* or on others. If you take this route, realise that you need to be in a healthy frame of mind to do this effectively and this is best achieved by dealing with your emotional problems about the *Situation* or about other(s).

If you are unsure about this, discuss it with your REBT therapist.

STEP 2

Assess a Concrete Example of Your Nominated Problem

2.1 Select a concrete example of your defined nominated problem

Once you have defined your nominated problem, select a concrete example of this problem. Working with a concrete example will help you to identify a specific *A* and a specific *C*, which will later help you to identify a specific rigid/extreme attitude (at *B*)

A concrete example occurs in a specific *Situation*, at a specific time and where a specific person or specific persons are present.

If you find it difficult to select a concrete example of your nominated problem, choose an example which is fresh in your mind. This example might be:

- Recent
- Vivid
- Typical

2.2 Describe the *Situation* as objectively as you can

Once you have chosen the concrete example of your nominated problem, describe the *Situation* in which you felt disturbed as specifically and objectively as you can. Such a description should contain no interpretations of what happened and, as such, is what can be seen and heard on an audio-visual record of the *Situation*.

For example:

- *Harry and Bill went to the football match and did not ask me if I wanted to go with them*
- *I told Jill that I had met a man and asked her not to tell anyone. She told Beryl about it*

2.3 Identify *C*

Identify how you felt in the *Situation* in question. Select one unhealthy negative emotion. If you felt several such emotions, identify the main one. If appropriate, identify your main dysfunctional behavioural response in the *Situation*.

Use the following:

**When .... (state the *Situation*) I felt...........
(state your unhealthy negative emotion)**

For example:

*When I told my mother I could not see her later today, and
she said, 'That's alright dear', I felt guilty.*

**When..................... (state the *Situation*) I ....
(state your dysfunctional behavioural response)**

For example:

*When I told my mother I could not see her later today, and
she said, 'That's alright dear', I cancelled my work meeting,
phoned her back and told her I was coming to see her after
all.*

Here are a few tips when you are identifying an emotional C:

- If your C is vague, specify it.
- Ensure that your C is unhealthy. See Table 2 (next page) for
  the nine most common unhealthy negative emotions for
  which people seek help. I have also included their healthy
  negative emotion alternatives.
- If you cannot see that your unhealthy negative emotion is
  unhealthy, discuss this with your REBT therapist.
- If you cannot identify an unhealthy negative emotion, select
  your major dysfunctional behaviour as your C.
- Keep a note of the reasons why you want to change C.

Table 2   The nine most common unhealthy negative emotions (UNEs) presented in therapy and their healthy negative emotion alternatives (HNEs)[4]

UNEs	HNEs
• Anxiety • Depression • Guilt • Shame • Hurt • Unhealthy anger • Unhealthy regret • Unhealthy jealousy • Unhealthy envy	• Concern • Sadness • Remorse • Disappointment • Sorrow • Healthy anger • Healthy regret • Healthy jealousy • Healthy envy

2.4   Identify *A*

You will recall from the introduction that I distinguish between *A* (the adversity in the *Situation* about which you were most disturbed) and the *Situation* in which you were disturbed. *A* is usually an inference, while the *Situation* is descriptive.

Here is a question that you can ask yourself to identify *A*:

---

[4] Please note that this list reflects the terminology that I tend to use. Developing a shared language with your therapist on this issue is more important than employing my language. The main point to remember is that at a suitable time, you need to discuss with your therapist what constitutes a healthy alternative to your UNE, given that your *A* is an adversity.

**What was I most …….. about (state your C) when ……….
(state the *Situation*)?**

For example:

• *What was I most angry about (C) when Kelly refused to
answer my question (Situation)*

If you struggle to answer this question, you might find it helpful
to use a technique called *Windy's Magic Question* (see next
page).

You may find Table 3 useful in helping to identify *A*. It lists
the themes of the adversity at *A* associated with the nine
unhealthy negative emotions cited above.

Once you have identified your *A*, it is very important that you
resist any temptation to challenge *A* even if it is obviously
distorted. Assume temporarily that your *A* is true. This will
enable you to identify your rigid/extreme attitude later along with
its flexible/non-extreme attitude alternative.

This is so important, let me repeat it:

Assume temporarily that your *A* is true

You will have an opportunity to re-examine your *A* later in
therapy and your REBT therapist will help you to do that.

Windy's Magic Question (WMQ)

Purpose: To help you to identify the *A* in the *ABC* framework as quickly as possible (i.e. what you are most disturbed about) once *C* has been assessed and the *Situation* in which *C* has occurred has been identified and briefly described.

Here, I use an example where a person is anxious about public speaking.

Step 1. Focus on your disturbed *C* (e.g. *anxiety*)

Step 2: Then, focus on the *Situation* in which *C* occurred (e.g. *about to give a public presentation to a group of consultants*)

Step 3: Ask yourself: *Which ingredient would I need to eliminate or significantly reduce C* (here, *anxiety*)? (In this case, the person said: *My mind not going blank*). Take care that you do not change the *Situation* (i.e. the person does not say: *Not giving the presentation*)

Step 4: The opposite is probably *A* (e.g. My mind going blank'), but check. The person asked themself: *So when I was about to give the presentation, was I most anxious about my mind going blank?* If not, use the question again until you confirm what you were most disturbed about in the described *Situation*.

2.5   Understand the *B–C* connection

At this point, you need to understand the *B-C* connection. In this context, this refers to REBT's view that your reactions (*C*) are not determined by the *Situation* or by your inference (*A*) but largely by your basic attitude (*B*). This is known as the *B-C* connection.

Table 3 Adversities at *A* related to unhealthy negative emotions at C^5

Adversity at *A*	Unhealthy Negative Emotion at *C*
• Threat	• Anxiety
• Loss • Failure • Undeserved plight (to self/others)	• Depression
• Breaking your moral code • Failing to live up to your moral code • Hurting/harming someone	• Guilt
• Something highly negative has been revealed about you (or about a group with whom you identify) by you or by others • Falling very short of your ideal • Others look down on or shun you (or a group with whom you identify)	• Shame
• Someone betrays you or lets you down, and you think you do not deserve such treatment • Another is not as invested in your relationship with them as you are	• Hurt
• You or another transgresses your personal rule • Another threatens your self-esteem • Frustration	• Unhealthy Anger
• Wishing you had not taken a course of action that you took • Wishing that you had taken a course of action that you didn't take	• Unhealthy Regret
• Threat to a valued relationship • Uncertainty related to that threat	• Unhealthy Jealousy
• Others have what you value and lack	• Unhealthy Envy

---

[5] Please note that the nine healthy negative emotions listed in Table 2 also relate to the same adversities. Thus, the threat is the adversity that features in both anxiety and concern.

Ask yourself:

Were my feelings of …….. (state *C*) determined by …… (state *A*) or by my attitude (*B*) towards ….. (state *A*)?

For example:

- *Were my feelings of guilt (C) determined by me upsetting Carol (A) or by my attitude towards upsetting Carol?*

If your answer shows that you understand the *B-C* connection, then you can proceed to the next step. If not, you can use the following method, known as the 100-person technique.

Would a hundred people of my age and gender all feel ….. (state *C*) about…… (state *A*)?

For example:

- *Would a hundred women aged 45 all feel guilty (C) if they had upset their friend (A)?*

If you say no, then you can probably see that the reason why 100 people have different feelings about *A* is that they have different attitudes towards *A*. Thus, you can see the *B–C* connection.

If you still cannot see the *B–C* connection, discuss this with your REBT therapist.

2.6   Identify your rigid/extreme attitude and see the flexible/non-extreme alternative to this attitude at *B*

At this point, you are ready to understand that your disturbed reactions at *C* are not determined by the *Situation* or by your inference at *A* but largely by your rigid/extreme attitude at *B*. There are several methods to help you see this. The one that I think is the most efficient is what I call *Windy's Review Assessment Procedure* (WRAP). I suggest it because it not only helps you to assess the specific rigid/extreme attitude in the selected example of your nominated problem, but it also helps you see what your flexible/non-extreme attitude is that will form the attitude-based solution to this problem. In using this method, I suggest that you identify your rigid attitude and the one extreme attitude that best accounts for your unhealthy negative emotion. In this example, I will assume that your nominated problem is guilt about upsetting your friend.

Windy's Review Assessment Procedure (WRAP)

1. Begin by reviewing what you know and what you don't know.

2. You know three things:

First, *you know that you felt guilt (C).*
Second, *you know you felt guilty about upsetting your friend (A).*
Third, *you know it is important that you don't upset your friend.*

---

3. You don't know:

Which of two attitudes your guilt was based on. So, when you felt guilty about upsetting your friend, was your guilt based on Attitude 1: It is important to me that I don't upset my friend and therefore I must not do so (Rigid attitude) or Attitude 2: It is important to me that I don't upset my friend, but that does not mean that I must not do so (Flexible attitude)?

4. If you can't see that your guilt was based on your rigid attitude, speak to your REBT therapist about it.

5. Once you know that your guilt was based on your rigid attitude, you understand the rigid attitude B – disturbed C connection. *Now, suppose instead that you had a strong conviction in attitude 2. How would you feel about upsetting your friend if you strongly believed that while it is important to you that you don't upset your friend, that does not mean that you must not do?*

6. If necessary, consult Table 2 and see that remorse is the healthy negative emotion alternative to guilt. Once you see this then you understand the flexible attitude B – healthy C connection.

7. At this point, you should understand the differences between the two *B–C* connections. If not, discuss this with your REBT therapist.

8. Set remorse as the emotional goal in this *Situation* and see that developing conviction in your flexible attitude is the best way of achieving this goal.

Once you have identified your rigid and flexible attitudes, you need to remind yourself of the other three extreme attitudes and their non-extreme attitude alternatives (listed in Table 1 in the section entitled REBT's *Situational ABCDE* Model of REBT above). Select the one extreme attitude that best accounted for your guilt (unhealthy negative emotion at *C*) and, by implication, the alternative non-extreme attitude that will help you to achieve your goal.

STEP 3

Prepare Yourself for the Attitude Examination Process

3.1   Understand that the first step to change your attitudes is to examine them

You have now identified your rigid/extreme attitude and its alternative flexible/non-extreme attitude and have understood the connection between the former and your unhealthy negative emotion (and/or dysfunctional behaviour) at *C* and the connection between the latter and the alternative healthy negative emotion (and/or functional behaviour) at *C*.

Now, you need to examine these two attitudes to determine which one you want to develop going forward. The first three points below review what you did at the end of Step 2.

- **State the two *B-C* connections**

For example:

I can see that if I hold a rigid/extreme attitude towards upsetting my friend I will feel guilt, but if I hold a flexible/non-extreme attitude towards this, I will feel remorse.

- **State your emotional goal**

For example:

I want to feel remorse about upsetting my friend and not guilt.

- **Understand that you need to change your rigid/extreme attitude to achieve this goal**

For example:

Given that holding a rigid/extreme attitude leads me to feel guilt and holding a flexible/non-extreme attitude would lead me to feel remorse, I need to change my rigid/extreme attitude to achieve my emotional goal.

If you can't see this, discuss the issue with your REBT therapist.

- **Understand that the first step in the attitude examination process involves you examining both attitudes so that you they can commit to one going forward.**

3.2   Guard against wanting to change *A* and not *B*

At this point, you may wish to change the adversity at *A* without changing your rigid/extreme attitude at *B* first. If this is the case, you need to see that the best time to change *A* is when you are *not* disturbed about *A* and that your disturbed feelings about *A* will interfere with your change attempts. Once you understand this and that the best way to be undisturbed about *A* is by holding a flexible/non-extreme attitude towards it, you are ready to engage in the attitude examination process.

If you have any remaining doubts about these points or reservations about committing yourself to change your attitude, discuss these with your REBT therapist.

STEP 4

Examine Your Attitudes

4.1   Understand that the purpose of examining your attitudes is for you to see that your rigid/extreme attitude is unhealthy and that your flexible/non-extreme attitude is healthy

When you examine your rigid/extreme and flexible/non-extreme attitudes, see that your rigid/extreme attitude is unhealthy (false, illogical, and yielding largely poor results) and your flexible/non-extreme attitude is healthy (true, logical and yielding largely good results). These characteristics are listed in Table 4 (next page). Strengthen your conviction in your flexible/non-extreme attitude and weaken your conviction in your rigid/extreme attitude is initiated in Step 5.

4.2   Examine both rigid/extreme and flexible/non-extreme attitudes together

As I said above, the purpose of examining your attitudes is to see that your rigid/extreme attitude is unhealthy (false, illogical and yields largely poor results and that your alternative flexible/non-extreme attitude is healthy (true, logical and yields largely good results). This is known as intellectual insight because while you may understand this point, you do not yet have deep conviction in it to the extent that it influences for the better your feelings and behaviour. This 'emotional insight' will come about in ongoing counselling, but work towards its achievement is initiated in Step 5.

Table 4   Characteristics of rigid/extreme attitudes and flexible/non-extreme attitudes

Rigid/Extreme Attitudes	Flexible/Non-Extreme Attitudes
• False • Illogical • Leads to unconstructive results	• True • Logical • Leads to constructive results

To achieve such intellectual insight, you must examine your rigid/extreme and flexible/non-extreme attitudes. While there are several ways of doing this, in my view, the most efficient way is for you to examine these attitudes together and I will outline this approach here.

In doing so, I suggest that you always examine your rigid and flexible attitudes (unless there is a good reason not to), as well as the *one* other extreme attitude that you resonate with the most, together with its non-extreme attitude alternative. The best way of doing this is to examine these two sets of attitudes separately, as shown below.

1. **Examine your rigid and flexible attitudes together. Always do this unless there is a good reason not to.**

2. **Separately, examine together the one extreme attitude with which you resonate with most and its non-extreme attitude alternative**

   - **Your unbearability and bearability attitudes**
   - **Your awfulising and non-awfulising attitudes**
   - **Your devaluation and unconditional acceptance attitudes**

4.3   Examine your rigid attitude and its flexible attitude alternative

Rigid Attitude	Flexible Attitude
• *I want (don't want) X to happen, and therefore it has to be the way I want it to be*	• *I want (don't want) X to happen, but it does not have to be the way I want it to be*

I recommend that you use three main questions when examining your rigid and flexible attitudes:

- The empirical question
- The logical question and
- The pragmatic question.

Then, you can select which attitude you want to strengthen, which you want to weaken, and why.

First, focus on your rigid attitude and its flexible attitude alternative. Write down both attitudes side by side (as above).[6]

Then, I will move on to the three questions. I will present them in a certain order. This order is only a guide, and other orders are fine.

4.3.1 The empirical question

Ask yourself: *Which of the following attitudes is true and which is false and why?*

- *My rigid attitude*
- *My flexible attitude*

According to REBT theory, the only correct answer to this question is that the flexible attitude is true and the rigid attitude is false. Thus:

- A rigid attitude is inconsistent with reality. For such a rigid attitude to be true the conditions that you are rigidly demanding to be present would already have to exist when they do not. Or, as soon as you make a rigid demand, these demanded conditions would have to exist. Both positions are patently inconsistent with reality.
- On the other hand, a flexible attitude is true since its two component parts are true. You can prove that you have a particular desire and can provide reasons why you want what

---

[6] Please note that, at this point, you will be working with your specific rigid and flexible attitudes.

you want. You can also prove that you do not have to get what you desire.

If you can't see this, discuss it with your REBT therapist.

4.3.2   The logical question

Ask yourself:

Which of the following attitudes is logical and which is illogical, and why?

- *My rigid attitude*
- *My flexible attitude*

You need to acknowledge that your rigid attitude is illogical while your flexible attitude is logical. See that your rigid attitude is based on the same desire as your flexible attitude, but that you transform it as follows:

- ***I want (don't want) X to happen, and therefore it has to be the way I want it to be***

Understand that this attitude has two components. The first [I want (don't want) X to happen] is not rigid, but the second [...and therefore it has to be the way I want it to be] is rigid. As such, your rigid attitude isn't logical since one cannot logically derive something rigid from something that is not rigid. The template in Figure 1 illustrates this visually.

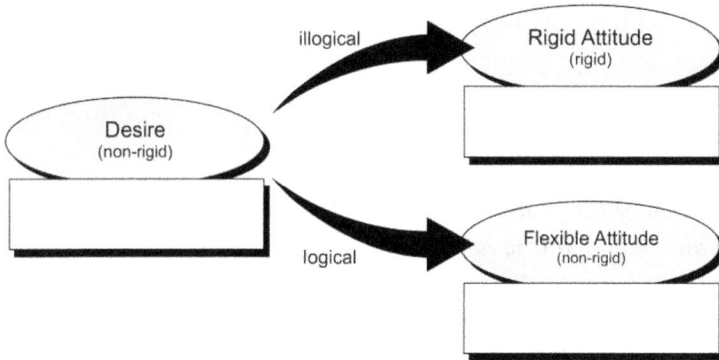

Figure 1: Examining the logical status of rigid and flexible attitudes

Your flexible attitude is as follows:

• *I want (don't want) X to happen, but it does not have to be the way I want it to be*

Your flexible attitude is logical since both parts are not rigid; thus, the second component logically follows from the first. Again, refer to the template in Figure 1 to see this visually, if necessary.

If you don't understand the correct answer, discuss it with your REBT therapist.

4.3.3   The pragmatic question

Ask yourself:

Which of the following attitudes leads to largely good results and which leads to largely poor results and why?

- *Your rigid attitude*
- *Your flexible attitude*

See that your rigid attitude leads to largely unconstructive results while your flexible attitude leads to more constructive ones. As you do this, use the information you provided in point 2.6.

If you think your rigid attitude leads to healthier consequences than your flexible attitude, discuss this with your REBT therapist.

4.3.4   Make a commitment to change your attitude

At this point, you need to make a commitment to change your attitude. You do this by asking yourself the following question:

Ask yourself:

Which attitude do I want to strengthen, and which do you want to weaken and why?

- *My rigid attitude*
- *My flexible attitude*

After you have examined your rigid and flexible attitudes, you 'should' indicate that you wish to work to strengthen your conviction in your flexible attitude and weaken your conviction in your rigid attitude and be able to give coherent reasons why, based on your problematic feelings and behaviour and your goals for change. If you doubt making such a commitment, discuss this with your REBT therapist.

4.4   Examine an awfulising attitude and its non-awfulising attitude alternative

Awfulising Attitude	Non-Awfulising Attitude
• *It would be bad if X happens (or does not happen), and therefore it would be terrible*	• *It would be bad if X happens (or does not happen), but it isn't terrible*

When examining your awfulising and non-awfulising attitudes, use the same three questions you used to examine your rigid and flexible attitudes: empirical, logical, and pragmatic. Once you have done this, ask yourself which attitude you want to strengthen, which you want to weaken, and why.

First, focus on your awfulising attitude and non-awfulising attitude. Again, write them down side by side (as above).[7] Then, move on to the three questions.

---

[7] Again, you will be working with your specific awfulising and non-awfulising attitudes.

4.4.1   The empirical question

Ask yourself:

Which of the following attitudes is true and which is false and why?

- *My awfulising attitude*
- *My non-awfulising attitude*

According to REBT theory, an awfulising attitude is false and a non-awfulising attitude is true.

While examining these attitudes, understand that when you are holding your awfulising attitude, you believe the following:

- Nothing could be worse;
- The event in question is worse than 100% bad
- No good could possibly come from this bad event
- You cannot transcend the event

See that all three convictions are inconsistent with reality and that your awfulising attitude is false. By contrast, see that your non-awfulising attitude is true since this is made up of the following ideas:

- Things could always be worse;
- The event in question is less than 100% bad
- Some good could come from this bad event
- You can transcend the event

If you give an answer that is at variance with the above, discuss this issue with your REBT therapist.

4.4.2 The logical question

Ask yourself:

Which of the following attitudes is logical and which is illogical, and why?

*   *My awfulising attitude*
*   *My non-awfulising attitude*

Understand that your awfulising attitude is illogical, while your non-awfulising attitude is logical. Your awfulising attitude is based on the same evaluation of badness as your non-awfulising attitude, but you transform this as follows:

It would be very bad if X happened (or did not happen) ..... *and therefore it would be terrible.*

Your awfulising attitude has two components. The first [It would be very bad if X happened (or did not happen)] is non-extreme, while the second (...and therefore it would be terrible) is extreme. As such, see that your awfulising attitude is illogical since one cannot logically derive something extreme from something that is not extreme. Figure 2 (next page) illustrates this point visually.

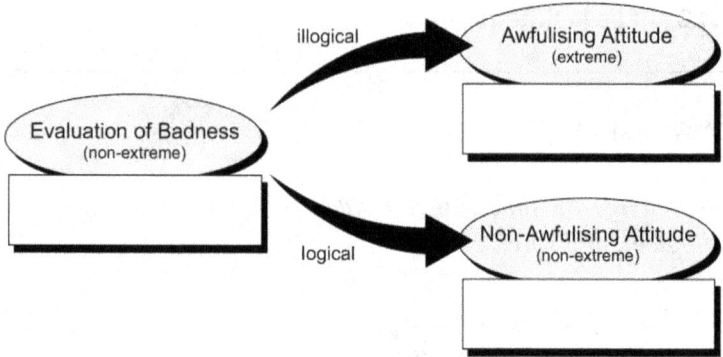

Figure 2: Examining the logical status of awfulising and non-awfulising attitudes

Your non-awfulising attitude is as follows:

> *It would be very bad if X happened (or did not happen) ... but it would not be terrible.*

See that your non-awfulising attitude is logical since both parts are non-extreme and thus the second component logically follows from the first. Again, Figure 2 illustrate this point visually.

4.4.3 The pragmatic question

Ask yourself:

Which of the following attitudes leads to largely good results and which leads to largely poor results and why?

- *My awfulising attitude*
- *My non-awfulising attitude*

See that your awfulising attitude leads to largely unconstructive results, while your non-awfulising attitude leads to more constructive ones. As you do this, use the information you provided in point 2.6.

If you think your awfulising attitude leads to healthier consequences than your flexible attitude, discuss this issue with your REBT therapist.

4.4.4 Make a commitment to change your attitude

At this point, you want to assess your commitment to change your attitude. You do this by asking the following question:

Ask yourself:

Which attitude do I want to strengthen, and which do I want to weaken and why?

- *My awfulising attitude*
- *My non-awfulising attitude*

After examining your awfulising and non-awfulising attitudes, you 'should' indicate that you wish to work to strengthen your conviction in your non-awfulising attitude and weaken your conviction in your awfulising attitude and be able to give coherent reasons why based on your problematic feelings and behaviour and their goals for change. If you give you any other answer, discuss this issue with your REBT therapist.

4.5   Examine your unbearability attitude and its bearability attitude alternative

Unbearability Attitude	Bearability Attitude
• *It would be a struggle for me to bear it if X happens (or does not happen, and therefore I could not bear it*	• *It would be a struggle for me to bear it if X happens (or does not happen), but I could bear it. It would be worth it to me to do so, and I am worth bearing it for. I am willing to bear it, and I am going to bear it.*

When examining your unbearability and bearability attitudes, use the same three questions you used to examine your rigid and flexible attitudes: the empirical, logical, and pragmatic. Once you have done this, you can ask yourself which attitude you want to strengthen, which you want to weaken, and why.

As before, begin by focusing on your unbearability attitude and your bearability attitude alternative. Write both attitudes down side by side (as above).[8] Then, move on to the three questions.

4.5.1   The empirical question

Ask yourself:

Which of the following attitudes is true and which is false and why?

- *My unbearability attitude*
- *My bearability attitude*

According to REBT theory, an unbearability attitude is false, and a bearability attitude is true.

While examining these attitudes, see that when you are holding your unbearability attitude, you believe the following:

- I will die or disintegrate if the adversity continues to exist
- I will lose the capacity to experience happiness if the adversity continues to exist.

See that both these convictions are inconsistent with reality and that your unbearability attitude is false. By contrast, see that your bearability attitude is true since this is made up of the following ideas:

---

[8] Yet again, you will be working with your specific unbearability and bearability attitudes.

- I will struggle if the adversity continues to exist, but I will neither die nor disintegrate;
- I will not lose the capacity to experience happiness if the adversity continues to exist, although this capacity will be temporarily diminished; and
- The adversity is worth bearing
- I am worth bearing the adversity for
- I am willing to bear it
- I am going to bear it

If you give an answer that is at variance with the above then discuss this with your REBT therapist.

4.5.2   The logical question

Ask yourself:

Which of the following attitudes is logical and which is illogical, and why?

- *My unbearability attitude*
- *My bearability attitude*

Acknowledge that your unbearability attitude is illogical while your bearability attitude is logical. See that an unbearability attitude is based on the same struggle component as your bearability flexible attitude, but that you transform it as follows:

It would be a struggle for me to bear it if X happened (or did not happen ... and therefore it would be unbearable

---

See that this attitude has two components. The first [It would be a struggle for me to bear it if *X* happened (or did not happen)] is not extreme, but the second [...and therefore it would be unbearable] is extreme. As such, your unbearability attitude isn't logical since one cannot logically derive something extreme from something that is not extreme rigid. Figure 3 illustrates this point visually.

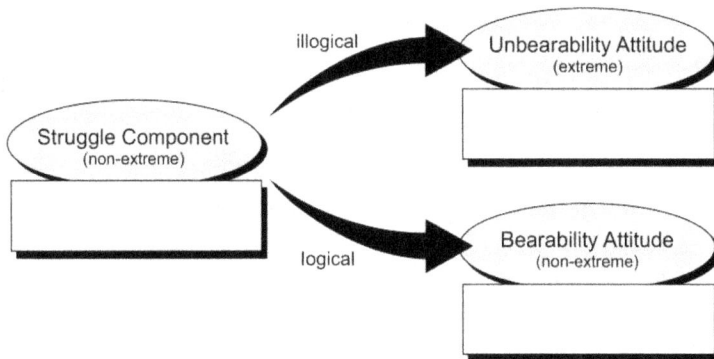

Figure 3: Examining the logical status of unbearability and bearability attitudes

Your bearability attitude is as follows:

- *It would be a struggle for me to bear it if X happens (or does not happen), but I could bear it. It would be worth it to me to do so, and I am worth bearing it for. I am willing to bear it, and I am going to bear it.*

Your bearability attitude is logical since all of its components are not extreme and are thus logically connected due to their non-extreme nature. Again, Figure 3 illustrates this point visually.

If you give any other answer, then discuss this issue with your REBT therapist.

4.5.3   The pragmatic question

Ask yourself:

Which of the following attitudes leads to largely good results and which leads to largely poor results and why?

- *My unbearability attitude*
- *My bearability attitude*

+

Acknowledge that your unbearability attitude leads to largely unconstructive results, while your bearability attitude leads to more constructive ones. As you do this, use the information you provided in point 2.6.

If you think your unbearability attitude leads to healthier consequences than your bearability attitude, discuss this issue with your REBT therapist.

4.5.4   Make a commitment to change your attitude

At this point, you need to make a commitment to change your attitude. You do this by asking yourself the following question:

Ask yourself:

Which attitude do you want to strengthen, and which do you want to weaken and why?

- *My unbearability attitude*
- *My bearability attitude*

After examining your unbearability and bearability attitudes, you 'should' indicate that you wish to work to strengthen your conviction in your bearability attitude and weaken your conviction in your unbearability attitude and be able to give coherent reasons why based on your problematic feelings and behaviour and your goals for change. Discuss this issue with your REBT therapist if you give any other answer.

4.6 Examine your devaluation attitude and its unconditional acceptance attitude alternative

Devaluation Attitude	Unconditional Acceptance Attitude
• If X happens (or does not happen), it proves that: - I am no good or - You are no good or - Life is no good	• If X happens (or does not happen), it does not prove that: - I am no good or - You are no good or - Life is no good It proves that: - I am a complex, unrateable fallible human being - You are a complex, unrateable human being - Life is a complex mixture of good, bad and neutral and is thus unrateable

When examining your devaluation and unconditional acceptance attitudes, again use the same three questions you used to examine your rigid and flexible attitudes: empirical, logical, and pragmatic. Once you have done this, you can ask which attitude you want to strengthen, which you want to weaken, and why.

Once again, focus on your devaluation attitude and its unconditional acceptance attitude alternative. As before, write both attitudes side by side (as above).[9] Then, move on to the three questions.

4.6.1   The empirical question

Ask yourself:

Which of the following attitudes is true and which is false and why?

- *My devaluation attitude*
- *My unconditional acceptance attitude*

According to REBT theory, an unconditional acceptance attitude is true, and a devaluation attitude is false.

4.6.1.1 Examine the empirical status of your person-devaluation (self- or other-) attitude and its unconditional acceptance attitude alternative

See that when you hold a person-devaluation attitude towards yourself or another person, you believe the following:

---

[9] As before, you will be working with their specific devaluation and unconditional acceptance attitudes.

- A person (self or other) can legitimately be given a single global rating that defines their essence and the worth of a person is dependent upon conditions that change (e.g. my worth goes up when I do well and goes down when I don't do well).
- A person can be rated based on one of their aspects.

Understand that these convictions are inconsistent with reality and that your person-devaluation attitude is false. By contrast, see that your unconditional acceptance attitude held towards yourself or another person is true since this is made up of the following ideas:

- A person cannot legitimately be given a single global rating that defines their essence and their worth, as far as they have it, is not dependent upon conditions that change (e.g. my worth stays the same whether or not I do well)
- It makes sense to rate discrete aspects of a person, but it does not make sense to rate a person based on these discrete aspects since the person is far too complex to merit such a rating

4.6.1.2 Examine the empirical status of their life-devaluation attitude and its unconditional acceptance attitude alternative

Understand that when you hold a life-devaluation attitude, you believe the following:

- The world can legitimately be given a single rating that defines its essential nature and that the value of the world varies according to what happens within it (e.g. the value of the world goes up when something fair occurs and goes down when something unfair happens)
- The world can be rated based on one of its aspects.

See that these convictions are inconsistent with reality and that your life-devaluation attitude is false. Further, see that your unconditional life-acceptance attitude is true since this is made up of the following ideas:

- Life cannot legitimately be given a single rating that defines its essential nature, and its value does not vary according to what happens within it (e.g. the value of life stays the same whether fairness exists at any given time or not).
- It makes sense to rate discrete aspects of life, but it does not make sense to rate life based on these discrete aspects since life is far too complex to merit such a rating.

If you give an answer that is at variance with the above, then discuss this issue with your REBT therapist.

4.6.2   The logical question

Ask yourself:

Which of the following attitudes is logical and which is logical and why?

- *My devaluation attitude*
- *My unconditional acceptance attitude*

Understand that their devaluation attitude is illogical, while their unconditional acceptance attitude is logical.[10]

For example, if you hold a self-devaluation attitude see that this attitude is based on the same idea as your unconditional self-

---

[10] The points in this section also apply to life-devaluation and unconditional life-acceptance attitudes.

acceptance attitude in that in both they acknowledge that it is bad if X happened, for example, but that you transform it as follows:

X is bad... and therefore I am bad

For example:

It would be bad if my boss criticises my report and if he does it proves I am worthless.

Here, your self-devaluation attitude has two components. The first (X is bad...) is your evaluation of a part of your experience, while the second (...and therefore I am bad) is your evaluation of the whole of your *self*. As such, you make an illogical part–whole error where the part is deemed illogically to define the whole.

Your unconditional self-acceptance attitude is as follows:

X is bad, but this does not mean that I am bad. I am a fallible human being even though X happened

For example:

It would be bad if my boss criticises my report. If he does, it does not prove I am worthless. I am the same unrateable, complex fallible human being whether he criticises my report or not.

Understand that your unconditional self-acceptance attitude is logical because it shows that your *self* is complex and incorporates a bad event. Thus, in holding your unconditional self-acceptance attitude, you avoid making the part–whole error.

4.6.3   The pragmatic question

Ask yourself:

Which of the following attitudes leads to largely good results and which leads to largely poor results and why?

• *My devaluation attitude*
• *My unconditional acceptance attitude*

Acknowledge that your devaluation attitude leads to largely unconstructive results, while your unconditional acceptance attitude leads to more constructive ones. As you do this, use the information you provided in point 2.6.

If you think your devaluation attitude leads to healthier consequences than their unconditional acceptance attitude, discuss this with your REBT therapist.

4.6.4   Make a commitment to change your attitude

At this point, you need to make a commitment to change your attitude. You do this by asking yourself the following question:

Ask yourself:

Which attitude do I want to strengthen, and which do I want to weaken and why?

- *My devaluation attitude*
- *My unconditional acceptance attitude*

After examining your devaluation and unconditional acceptance attitudes, you 'should' indicate that you wish to work to strengthen your conviction in your unconditional acceptance attitude and weaken your conviction in your devaluation attitude and be able to give coherent reasons why based on your problematic feelings and behaviour and your goals for change. Discuss this issue with your REBT therapist if you give any other answer.

STEP 5

Strengthen Your Conviction in Your Flexible/Non-Extreme Attitudes and Weaken Your Conviction in Your Rigid/Extreme Attitudes

While a full discussion of how you can strengthen your conviction in your flexible/non-extreme attitude and weaken your conviction in your rigid/extreme attitude is beyond the scope of this brief book, I will suggest two ways you can do so to initiate this process.

5.1   Use rational-emotive imagery

Rational-emotive imagery (REI) is an imagery method designed to help you practise changing your *specific* rigid/extreme attitude to its flexible/non-extreme alternative while simultaneously imagining what you are most disturbed about in the specific *Situation* in question. This method will help you to strengthen your conviction in your new flexible/non-extreme attitude.

What follows is a set of instructions for using REI.

5.1.1   Instructions for using REI

*   Take a *Situation* in which you disturbed yourself and identify the aspect of the *Situation* you were most disturbed about.
*   Close your eyes and imagine the *Situation* as vividly as possible and focus on the adversity at *A*.
*   Allow yourself to really experience the unhealthy negative emotion that you felt at the time while still focusing intently on the *A*. Ensure that your unhealthy negative emotion is *one* of the following: anxiety, depression, shame, guilt, hurt, unhealthy regret, unhealthy anger, unhealthy jealousy, and unhealthy envy.
*   Really experience this disturbed emotion for a moment or two and then change your emotional response to a healthy negative emotion, while all the time focusing intently on the adversity at *A*. Do not change the intensity of the emotion, just the emotion. Thus, if your original unhealthy negative emotion was anxiety, change this to concern; if it was depression, change it to sadness. Change shame to disappointment, guilt to remorse, hurt to sorrow, unhealthy regret to healthy regret. unhealthy anger to healthy anger, unhealthy jealousy to healthy jealousy and unhealthy envy to healthy envy. Again, change the unhealthy negative emotion to its healthy equivalent, but keep the level of intensity of the new emotion as strong as the old emotion. Keep experiencing this new emotion for about five minutes, always focusing on the adversity at *A*. If you go back to the old, unhealthy negative emotion, bring the new healthy negative emotion back.
*   At the end of five minutes, ask yourself how you changed your emotion.
*   Make sure that you changed your emotional response by changing your specific rigid/extreme attitude to flexible/non-extreme alternative. If you did not do so (if, for example, you changed your emotion by changing *A* to make it less negative or neutral or by holding an indifference attitude towards *A*),

do the exercise again and keep doing this until you have changed your emotion only by changing your specific rigid/extreme attitude to flexible/non-extreme alternative.

Practise REI several times a day and aim for 30 minutes daily practice when you are not doing any other therapy homework. If you have any problems using REI discuss them with your REBT therapist.

5.2   Rehearse your flexible/extreme attitudes while acting in ways that are consistent with these attitudes

Perhaps the most powerful way of strengthening your flexible/non-extreme attitude is to rehearse it while facing the relevant adversity at *A* and while acting in ways that are consistent with this attitude. Think of ways that help you to implement the above principle.

When your behaviour and attitude are in sync and you keep them in sync, you maximise the chances of strengthening your conviction in your flexible/non-extreme attitude. Refrain from acting and thinking in ways that are consistent with your old rigid/extreme attitude.

Use the following reminder when setting yourself behavioural-cognitive homework tasks:

Face the adversity at *A* + Rehearse the flexible/non-extreme attitude at *B* + Act in ways consistent with this flexible/non-extreme attitude.

Your REBT therapist will also help you to devise and monitor such homework assignments.

Appendix 1

Use an REBT Self-Help Form

Many REBT therapists suggest that their clients use a written self-help form in assessing their problems and intervening in them. I have included the self-help form that I use because it approximates the steps that I have discussed in this book and contains its own instructions for use. Feel free to experiment with its use.

REBT Self-Help Form

Situation =	
Adversity (*A*) =	

Basic Attitudes (*B*) (Rigid and Extreme)	Basic Attitudes (*B*) (Flexible and Non-Extreme)
Rigid = *Extreme* =	*Flexible* = *Non-Extreme* =
Consequences (*C*) (Unhealthy and Unconstructive) *Emotional* = *Behavioural* = *Thinking* =	Goals (*G*) (Healthy and Constructive) *Emotional* = *Behavioural* = *Thinking* =

INSTRUCTIONS (with reference to the previous page)

1. Write down a brief, objective description of the *Situation* you were in.
2. Identify your *C* - your major disturbed emotion, your unconstructive behaviour and, if relevant, your distorted and/or ruminative subsequent thinking.
3. Identify your *A* - this is what you were most disturbed about in the *Situation* (Steps 2 and 3 are interchangeable).
4. Set emotional, behavioural and thinking goals at *G*.
5. Identify your rigid/extreme basic attitude i.e. rigid attitude + awfulising attitude, unbearability attitude or devaluation attitude.
6. Identify the alternative flexible/non-extreme basic attitudes that will enable you to achieve your goals, i.e. flexible attitude + non-awfulising attitude, bearability attitude or unconditional acceptance attitude.

INSTRUCTIONS (with reference to the following page)

7. Examine (at *D*) both your rigid/extreme attitudes and flexible/non-extreme attitudes and choose one set to operate on. Give reasons for your choice. Which set would you teach a group of children, for example and why? Remember that you are choosing attitudes that will help you to achieve your emotional, behavioural and thinking goals. The effects of dialectical examination (or *E* should be your goals at *G*.
8. List the actions you are going to take to achieve your goals
9. Examine *A* and consider how realistic it was. Given all the facts, would there have been a more realistic way of looking at *A*? – if so, write it down.

D (Dialectical Examination) =

Taking Action =

Examine *A* =

Index

63

Feedback Request

You have now reached the end of the guide. I would appreciate feedback on your experiences using it so that I may improve subsequent editions. Feel free to email me at windy@windydryden.com

Windy Dryden

London & Eastbourne, December 2024

www.ingramcontent.com/pod-product-compliance
Lightning Source LLC
Chambersburg PA
CBHW060634280326
41933CB00012B/2040